W_ Inside?

written by
Karen Hoenecke
illustrated by
Bruce Biddle

Let's take a look inside.

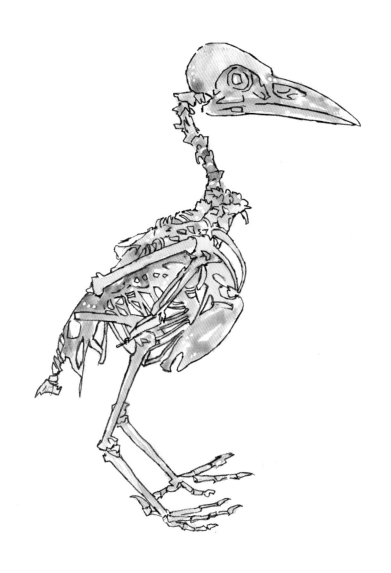

These bones belong to...

...a bird.

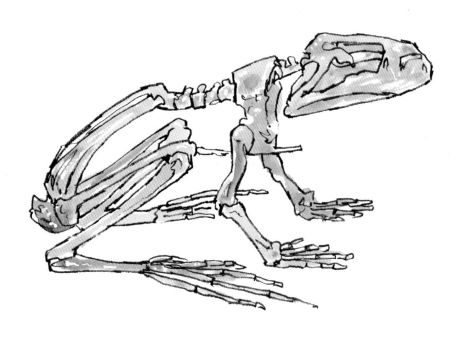

These bones belong to...

...a frog.

These bones belong to...

...a rabbit.

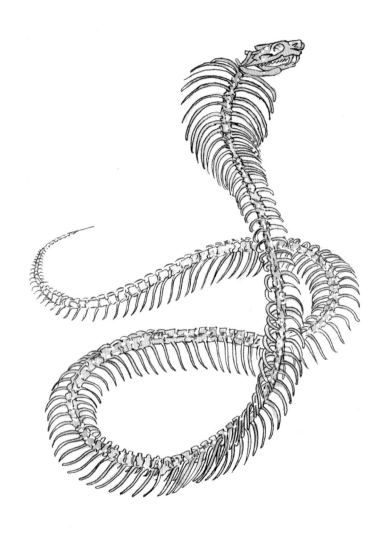

These bones belong to...

...a snake.

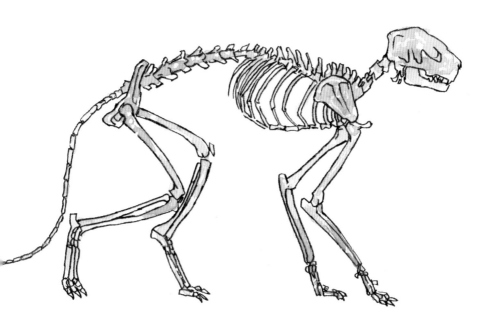

These bones belong to...

...a cat.

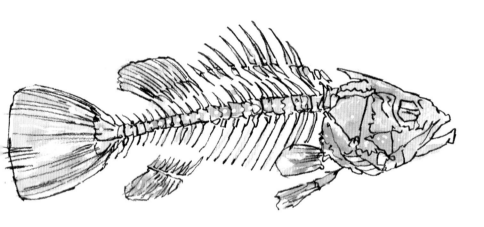

These bones belong to...

...a fish.

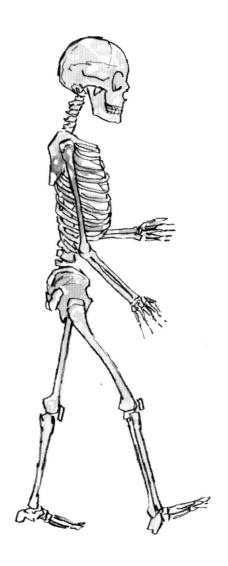

These bones belong to...

...a person.